my
baby
book

Starring me _____, the baby!

with supporting roles played by

_____ and _____
(my mom and dad)

conceived (so to speak) by
amy krouse rosenthal

potter style

Potter Style is a trademark and Potter and colophon are registered trademarks of Random House, Inc.

ISBN 978-0-307-46542-9

Printed in China

www.potterstyle.com

Cover design by Jim Massey

Interior design by Karla Baker

10 9 8 7 6 5 4 3 2 1

First Edition

my baby book

Well, by the looks of me, it's official: *I'm a baby!*

And by the looks of what is in your hand, this is officially *My Baby Book!*

I may not know much yet, but I do know this: We're going to enjoy romping through this journal together. Indeed, that is the whole point.

Take a glance at the three sections. You'll see that they are logically and chronologically arranged:

1. **my arrival:** Details about how I got here and the scoop on my family background.

2. **my first year:** A brief written snapshot of my life each month with allotted slots for see-me-grow photographs.

3. **my gallery of firsts:** A collection of moments, milestones, and sundry achievements throughout this big year.

Bottom line: This is meant to be a zero-pressure, zero-stress endeavor. If we need to skip pages, we'll skip pages! If a detail is forgotten, oh well! I assure you right here and now that a partially filled-out baby book will still be a treasured keepsake for all involved.

Thank you in advance for filling this out for me.

And thank you (nine months after the fact) for, well, filling out for me.

note to parent:

For the sake of brevity and simplicity, this book uses the "mom and dad" paradigm, but we hope the many single parent families, two-mom families, and two-dad families will enjoy this book just the same (and make the text adjustments accordingly).

my arrival

my folks
(pre-me)

insert photo here

In this picture, Mom is

☐ _____ weeks pregnant (and knows it).

☐ _____ weeks pregnant (and has no clue).

☐ many weeks away from being pregnant.

(See the glimmer in her eye? That would be me.)

from where did I come?

Here are some vital stats about
the two fine folks who made me.

mommy   ## daddy

aka: _____   aka: _____
(mother's name)   (father's name)

Birthday: _____   Birthday: _____

_____   _____

Place of birth: _____   Place of birth: _____

_____   _____

Current job: _____   Current job: _____

_____   _____

Especially good at: _____   Especially good at: _____

_____   _____

Not particularly good at: _____   Not particularly good at: _____

_____   _____

She hopes I will inherit her: ____   He hopes I will inherit his: ____

_____   _____

They believe in:

☐ truth   ☐ serendipity   ☐ God

☐ some higher power ☐ flossing   ☐ magic

☐ chocolate   ☐ me

breaking the
big news

How/when Mom confirmed that I was indeed on the way:

_____

_____

_____

How she broke the news to Dad (and what he said):

_____

_____

_____

The first people who were told about my imminent arrival (and what they said):

_____

_____

_____

Realizing that they would soon be wholly responsible for another human being for the rest of their natural born lives, my parents felt:

☐ excited   ☐ overwhelmed   ☐ overjoyed

☐ scared   ☐ unprepared   ☐ honored

☐ ready   ☐ shocked   ☐ grateful

ultra-amazing

insert ultrasound photo here

Date: _____

At this point, my folks know that I am going to be:

☐ a girl   ☐ a boy   ☐ a they (twins!)   ☐ a total surprise

This being their first glimpse of me, here's what went through their minds that day:

_____

_____

already loving
the attention

Additional photos of the in-utero me . . .

it's raining . . .
baby gear

Here are some of the most memorable, sentimental, and/or instrumental gifts:

_____ from _____

_____ from _____

_____ from _____

_____ from _____

_____ from _____

_____ from _____

_____ from _____

_____ from _____

_____ from _____

_____ from _____

_____ from _____

_____ from _____

_____ from _____

_____ from _____

_____ from _____

**Photos and/or memorabilia from my baby shower,
given by _____ on _____**

drawing a blank

I know it's hard to remember what life was like before my arrival. (Freedom? What's that again?!) Use these two blank pages to sketch, doodle, or jot down anything you want about life pre-me (weekend routines, favorite restaurants, general flow of life, etc.).

hello, world—
i'm here!

I arrived . . .

☐ _____ days before my due date. (I just couldn't wait any longer!)

☐ _____ days past my due date. (It was so cozy in there!)

☐ right on time.

☐ right on time with some inducement to help me along.

Not to *belabor* the issue . . .

But it took me and Mom _____ hours of hard work to get here. Thanks, Mom!

Exact date and time of my arrival: _____

Where I was born: _____

Who delivered me: _____

Who else was present: _____

_____

How Mom and Dad felt holding me for the first time:

_____

_____

Other interesting details about my birth:

_____

_____

quick. can you
spot me in this picture?

insert photo here

One of our very first photos. Date: _____

My eyes are:

☐ blue ☐ gray ☐ green ☐ brown ☐ hazel ☐ not sure yet

My hair is: ☐ blond ☐ brown ☐ black ☐ red

☐ abundant ☐ nonexistent

I weigh _____ lbs. _____ oz., and I am _____ inches long.

all about **moi**

My full name: _____

Why it was chosen: _____

_____

_____

Other names that Mom and Dad considered: _____

_____

_____

My nicknames: _____

_____

_____

My birthmark(s): _____

_____

_____

People say I look like: _____

_____

_____

Please don't hold me to birth order stereotypes, but I am the

_____ born in the family.

how the
stars alligned
for me

Capricorn–The Goat–December 22–January 19

Aquarius–The Water Carrier–January 20–February 18

Pisces–The Fish–February 19–March 20

Aries–The Ram–March 21–April 19

Taurus–The Bull–April 20–May 20

Gemini–The Twins–May 21–June 21

Cancer–The Crab–June 22–July 22

Leo–The Lion–July 23–August 22

Virgo–The Virgin–August 23–September 22

Libra–The Scales–September 23–October 23

Scorpio–The Scorpion–October 24–November 21

Sagittarius–The Archer–November 22–December 21

My astrological sign: _____

My mother's sign: _____

My father's sign: _____

What do the stars say about our compatibility?

_____

_____

birthday flowers

January–Carnation, Snowdrop

February–Violet, Primrose

March–Daffodil, Jonquil

April–Daylily, Sweet Pea

May–Lily of the Valley, Hawthorn

June–Rose, Honeysuckle

July–Larkspur, Water Lily

August–Gladiola, Poppy

September–Aster, Morning Glory

October–Calendula, Cosmos

November–Chrysanthemum

December–Narcissus, Holly

My birthday flower: _____

birthstones and their meaning

January–Garnet (Constancy)

February–Amethyst (Sincerity)

March–Aquamarine (Courage)

April–Diamond, White Sapphire (Innocence)

May–Emerald (Love, Success)

June–Pearl, Moonstone, Alexandrite (Health and Longevity)

July–Ruby (Contentment)

August–Peridot, Sardonyx (Married Happiness)

September–Sapphire (Clear Thinking)

October–Opal, Tourmaline, Pink Sapphire (Hope)

November–Topaz, Citrine (Fidelity)

December–Blue Topaz, Zircon (Prosperity)

My birthstone: _____

Of course, most of all, *I'm* your little gem.

my cute feet!

insert prints here

my teeny
hands!

My handprints (or a tracing of my little hand)

my birth
announcement

A copy of the printed announcement or e-mail that went around

insert announcement here

precious
mementos
(emphasis on me!)

Tape hospital bracelets, pressed flowers, favorite cards, notes, or photos on these pages.

i dig it here

**My new home is so much more spacious
than where I've been the last nine months!**

My address is: _____

_____

_____

Mom and Dad have lived here for _____ years.

Other kid(s) in the household are [name(s) and age(s)]:

_____

_____

_____

The household pet(s):

_____

_____

Friends and relatives who live nearby:

_____

_____

My room used to be a _____

Here's how my folks redecorated it for me:

_____

_____

homecoming

Here we are coming home together for the first time.

⌐   ¬

insert photo here

∟   ⌐

Date: _____

Random thoughts I want to be sure we remember about this big day:

_____

_____

_____

parental
boot camp

How I trained you to be Mom and Dad in no time!

Here's how the breastfeeding shook down (sorry, bad choice of words):

_____

_____

_____

Actually, we decided bottle feeding was preferable for us. Here's why:

_____

_____

_____

Wow, you should have seen my first poop! Oh, right—you did! It occurred:

_____

Who changes my diapers most? I'd have to say:

☐ Mom   ☐ Dad   ☐ That's a loaded question.

Mom manages to get a shower in:

☐ first thing in the morning.   ☐ by five in the afternoon.

☐ if we're having company.

the crying spectrum:
here's where i currently fall

Not very much ━━━━━━━━━━━━━━━━━━ **Incessantly**
(if you must know)

You guys know just how to comfort me by:

☐ swaddling me   ☐ rocking me   ☐ driving me around the block

☐ singing these songs: _____

☐ playing this music: _____

☐ This may sound crazy, but what really works is:

_____

_____

Who gets up with me in the middle of the night the most?

☐ Mom   ☐ Dad   ☐ They take turns

☐ Neither; we're all sleeping like babies!

☐ I plead the fifth, whatever that means.

While my folks got accustomed to the newness of my existence, they had
some help from:

_____

_____

_____

let's take a
second to talk
about some firsts

(Mom, Dad: Please don't stress if you can't remember the exact dates. Approximate dates work just as well.)

My first bath: _____

Who bathed me: _____

My umbilical cord fell off: _____

My first excursion out of house: _____

We went _____

_____

_____

_____

First time you went out without me! _____

Who babysat: _____

What did you do? _____

_____

_____

_____

This is a big one: My first smile! _____

celebrating
my arrival

My spiritual life began with this ceremony:

☐ christening   ☐ bris

☐ other religious/spiritual ritual: _____

Where it took place:

_____

_____

_____

Who led it:

_____

_____

_____

Who attended:

_____

_____

_____

I was bestowed with these nice gifts:

_____

_____

_____

photos and memorabilia from this special day

my godparents

The special people who were selected by my parents:

_____

_____

insert photo here

my family
mom's side

My grandparents' names are: But I will probably call them:

➡ _____

➡ _____

➡ _____

➡ _____

➡ _____

I know how excited my grandparents are about my arrival because they've said so, right here:

_____

_____

_____

Mom's siblings are:

_____

_____

_____

My cousins are:

_____

_____

_____

I am the _____ grandchild on this side of the family.

**Pictures of me with relatives from my mom's
side of the family . . .**

my family
dad's side

My grandparents' names are: But I will probably call them:

➡ _____

➡ _____

➡ _____

➡ _____

➡ _____

In their words, here's how they feel about being grandparents:

_____

_____

_____

Dad's siblings are:

_____

_____

_____

My cousins are:

_____

_____

_____

I am the _____ grandchild on this side of the family.

**Pictures of me with relatives from my dad's
side of the family . . .**

my first year
month by month

note to parents:

It might be fun to perch me on the same couch or chair or with the same stuffed animal for these monthly snapshots. Over the course of the year, as the backdrop stays the same, it will be easy to see how I've grown.

snapshot of my life
at 1 month

insert photo here

Date: _____

Stats (height/weight if handy, or any other interesting details): _____

My longest sleeping stretch at this point is _____ hours.

I'd have to say the cutest thing I've done so far is: _____

_____

About this period of time, we want to be sure to remember this: _____

_____

_____

snapshot of my life
at 2 months

insert photo here

Date: _____

Stats (height/weight if handy, or any other interesting details): _____

My longest sleeping stretch at this point is _____ hours.

I'd have to say the cutest thing I've done so far is: _____

_____

About this period of time, we want to be sure to remember this:

_____

_____

snapshot of my life
at 3 months

insert photo here

Date: _____

Stats (height/weight if handy, or any other interesting details): _____

My longest sleeping stretch at this point is _____ hours.

I'd have to say the cutest thing I've done so far is: _____

_____

About this period of time, we want to be sure to remember this:

_____

_____

exclusive
interview: **3** months

Interviewer: **me** (the baby)

Interviewee(s): **mom and dad**

Date: _____

So, I've been around for about three months now. Are you blown away by the amount of work I require, or were you mentally prepared for all of this?

_____

What is your favorite time of day with me? _____

What's the first thing you do when I'm asleep? _____

_____

Since I arrived, I've been helping you meet other people with new babies. What do you think of this new scene? _____

_____

What's the best piece of parenting advice you've received so far? The worst? _____

_____

Go ahead, be honest. How would you describe my budding personality? _____

_____

What is the strangest thing that you've done in a sleep-deprived state? _____

_____

snapshot of my life
at 4 months

insert photo here

Date: _____

Stats (height/weight if handy, or any other interesting details): _____

My longest sleeping stretch at this point is _____ hours.

I'd have to say the cutest thing I've done so far is: _____

_____

About this period of time, we want to be sure to remember this:

_____

_____

snapshot of my life
at 5 months

insert photo here

Date: _____

Stats (height/weight if handy, or any other interesting details): _____

My longest sleeping stretch at this point is _____ hours.

I'd have to say the cutest thing I've done so far is: _____

_____

About this period of time, we want to be sure to remember this:

_____

_____

snapshot of my life at 6 months

insert photo here

Date: _____

Stats (height/weight if handy, or any other interesting details): _____

My longest sleeping stretch at this point is _____ hours.

I'd have to say the cutest thing I've done so far is: _____

_____

About this period of time, we want to be sure to remember this:

_____

_____

exclusive
interview: **6 months**

Interviewer: **me** (the baby)

Interviewee(s): **mom and dad**

Date: _____

OK, so I am half a year old. Have you been having date nights yet? If so, what did you do?

_____

_____

How much did you end up talking about me? _____

Are both of you back at work now? If so, how do you feel about that?

_____

_____

Do you think that having me has brought you closer to your own families?

_____

_____

What are some of your favorite things we do together?

_____

_____

You know how much I love you. How would you describe the love you feel for me?

_____

_____

snapshot of my life
at 7 months

insert photo here

Date: _____

Stats (height/weight if handy, or any other interesting details): _____

My longest sleeping stretch at this point is _____ hours.

I'd have to say the cutest thing I've done so far is: _____

_____

About this period of time, we want to be sure to remember this:

_____

_____

snapshot of my life
at 8 months

insert photo here

Date: _____

Stats (height/weight if handy, or any other interesting details): _____

My longest sleeping stretch at this point is _____ hours.

I'd have to say the cutest thing I've done so far is: _____

_____

About this period of time, we want to be sure to remember this:

_____

_____

snapshot of my life
at 9 months

insert photo here

Date: _____

Stats (height/weight if handy, or any other interesting details): _____

My longest sleeping stretch at this point is _____ hours.

I'd have to say the cutest thing I've done so far is: _____

_____

About this period of time, we want to be sure to remember this:

_____

_____

snapshot of my life
at 10 months

insert photo here

Date: _____

Stats (height/weight if handy, or any other interesting details): _____

My longest sleeping stretch at this point is _____ hours.

I'd have to say the cutest thing I've done so far is: _____

_____

About this period of time, we want to be sure to remember this:

_____

_____

snapshot of my life at 11 months

insert photo here

Date: _____

Stats (height/weight if handy, or any other interesting details): _____

My longest sleeping stretch at this point is _____ hours.

I'd have to say the cutest thing I've done so far is: _____

_____

About this period of time, we want to be sure to remember this:

_____

_____

exclusive
interview : **12** months

Questions for my folks on their first anniversary of being parents. Congratulations, by the way!

Can you believe I'm veering toward toddler-hood? Do you feel nostalgic looking back on my first year?

_____

How have things gotten easier since I was first born?

_____

What do you find the most challenging?

_____

Do you think you'll want to have another baby based on your experience with me?

_____

What's the most surprising thing you've learned about yourself as a parent?

_____

How would you describe me in 1,000 words or less? (Kidding. A sentence or two will do.)

_____

_____

i am officially . . .
one
awesome baby!

insert photo here

my birthday!

insert photo here

happy 1st birthday to me!

How we celebrated:

_____

_____

Who was there:

_____

_____

My birthday cake was:

_____

_____

What I thought of it:

_____

_____

My favorite gifts:

_____

_____

It was a great day for sure. But this part was the icing on the cake:

_____

_____

photos from the
party

1st birthday cards and mementos

Here is my birthday invitation, some favorite cards, and other souvenirs from my first birthday party.

these are a few of my
favorite things

My favorite toy: _____

My favorite stuffed animal: _____

My favorite blanket: _____

My favorite books: _____

My favorite games: _____

My favorite movies or shows: _____

My favorite park: _____

My favorite thing to do at the park: _____

My favorite songs: _____

My favorite foods: _____

My favorite outfit: _____

My favorite pals: _____

My favorite _____ : _____

note to parent:

Mom, Dad, I know I keep you *plenty* busy. And so please, do not worry about documenting each and every milestone of my first year. Unless you want to be in the Parental Hall of Fame, then, yes, you should fill out every single page in this section. Remember, have fun! I know I am!

my first
full night of sleep

I started sleeping through the night when . . .

☐ I was _____ weeks/months old.

☐ Um, this actually hasn't happened with any consistency yet. I'm terribly sorry.

FYI, my nap time(s) is: _____

My bed time is: _____

I usually wake up at: _____

Our bedtime routine is:

_____

_____

_____

_____

_____

_____

ha! ha! ha!ppiness!

I cracked my first smile when I was _____ weeks old. (You could say this was a major *smile*stone.)

_____ made me laugh for the first time.

When Mom and Dad want to make me laugh, they will do just about anything including:

_____

_____

_____

_____

_____

When I want to make Mom and Dad laugh, this is what I do:

_____

_____

_____

_____

_____

_____

say (macaroni and) cheese!

An especially smiley photo of me . . .

insert photo

my first
bath

When my bare behind first hit the water, I was:

☐ excited   ☐ curious   ☐ angry   ☐ relaxed

When my mom/dad first handled my slippery little body, she/he felt:

☐ confident   ☐ clumsy   ☐ anxious   ☐ amused

Now that I can sit up and splash around, this is how I feel about bath time:

_____

_____

_____

_____

My favorite bath toys, games, and songs are:

_____

_____

_____

_____

After my bath, Mom thinks that I smell like: _____

bathing beauty

Rub-a-dub-dub, that's me in the tub . . .

insert photo here

my first
hair cut

(tape lock of hair here)

insert photo here

Who cut my hair: _____

I was: ☐ excited   ☐ happy   ☐ sad · ☐ fussy   ☐ calm

my first
tooth

I started teething when I was: _____

My mood changed in the following ways: _____

_____

_____

Luckily, you did this to alleviate my discomfort:

_____

_____

My first tooth appeared on: _____

insert photo here

tasty firsts

First time I held my own bottle: _____

First time I ate baby food: _____

First time I ate solid food: _____

First time I fed myself: _____

First time I used a sippy cup: _____

Foods I seem to love: _____

_____

_____

Foods I seem to loathe: _____

_____

_____

By the way, about that breastfeeding:

☐ We stopped at _____ months. ☐ We're still going strong at _____ months.

Overall, I am a: ☐ picky eater ☐ hearty eater ☐ typical, I suppose

My parents' philosophy about cooking, food, and family meals:

_____

_____

my first words

First time I said "dada": _____

First time I said "mama": _____

A sampling of some of my other early words:

_____

_____

My first phrase or sentence:

_____

_____

Luckily, you oblige by speaking my language, too. For example, you'll say:

_____ because that's how I understand "bottle."

_____ because that's how I understand "blanket."

_____ because that's how I understand "pacifier."

_____ because that's how I understand "food."

_____ because that's how I understand _____

_____ because that's how I understand _____

_____ because that's how I understand _____

_____ because that's how I understand

i'm a mover
and a shaker

First time I rolled over: _____

First time I really shook a rattle: _____

First time I crawled: _____

When and where my first steps occurred:

_____

_____

_____

_____

_____

How my parents' lives have changed now that I'm getting around on my own:

_____

_____

_____

_____

_____

one small step for baby...
one GIANT leap toward
baby-proofing everything.

A photo of me on the move.

insert photo here

my sweetest gestures

First time I waved hello and/or good-bye (who was I waving to?):

_____

_____

First time I played peek-a-boo (with whom?):

_____

_____

First time I gave a kiss (who was the lucky recipient?):

_____

_____

_____

First book I asked for/pointed to:

_____

_____

_____

my first
drawing

Draw on this blank page.

Some may call it abstract art (others call it a scribble), but I think this looks like a:

first big trip

I hit the road with my folks for our first major trip together when I was: _____
months old.

Where we went: _____

Why we went: _____

_____

_____

_____

What we did: _____

_____

_____

_____

_____

True or False? After this first travel experience, Mom and Dad are eager to do it again. Why or why not?

_____

_____

_____

_____

precious cargo

A photo of me strapped in and ready to roll on my first big voyage.

insert photo

first
mother's day

insert photo

This is what Dad and I did to let Mom know how much I love her:

_____

_____

_____

first
father's day

insert photo

This is what Mom and I did to let Dad know how much I love him:

_____

_____

_____

my first **spring**

insert photo

On the first official day of spring of my first year, I was _____ months old.

This is how we kept the spring in our step this season:

_____

_____

_____

_____

my first summer

insert photo

On the first official day of summer of my first year, I was _____ months old.

Some things we did to savor summer together:

_____

_____

_____

_____

my first swim

insert photo

I went for my first dip when I was about _____ months old.

I say it was just one enormous bathtub. Others might call it:

☐ a lake   ☐ an ocean   ☐ a swimming pool   ☐ a kiddie pool

How did I react to this vast watery-ness?

_____

_____

my first **autumn**

insert photo

On the first official day of autumn of my first year, I was _____ months old.

Some things we did together as leaves (and I) continued to change:

_____

_____

_____

my first halloween

Orange and black(mail) anyone?

insert photo

My mom enjoys putting me in lots of different outfits, but this is the strangest get-up yet. For my first

Halloween, I was costumed as a(n): _____.

I acted the part by: _____

_____

_____

_____

my first
thanksgiving

insert photo

Another new ritual._____
(names of family members)

all got together at _____

to eat _____

I participated by eating _____ and expressing

my gratitude for everything in my little life by: _____

_____

my first winter

insert photo

On the first official day of winter of my first year, I was _____ months old.

How we enjoyed this winter wonderland together:

_____

_____

_____

_____

my first **big holiday**

insert photo

I've learned that since we are _____ (religious orientation), we celebrate

_____ at the end of the year.

I think that I'm going to be looking forward to this day for years to come. Here's how we celebrated.

Where we went: _____

Who else was there: _____

How I personally participated in the festivities: _____

_____

first **family** **holiday** card

Starring yours truly, of course!

insert photo/card

a couple **firsts** that are **unique** to our family . . .

Date: _____

First: _____

_____

_____

Date: _____

First: _____

_____

_____

Date: _____

First: _____

_____

_____

Date: _____

First: _____

_____

_____

Date: _____

First: _____

_____

_____

_____

Date: _____

First: _____

_____

_____

_____

Date: _____

First: _____

_____

_____

_____

Date: _____

First: _____

_____

_____

_____

a letter from
mommy and daddy

You can write about just about anything that comes to mind. For example, what a typical day is like for us; what I'm like after one year on Earth; something funny/interesting I've said or done lately. I look forward to reading this one day. And thank you in advance!

the last word

Us kids always seem to want get in the last word, right? Why should my own baby book be any different?! Let's save this last page as a place to return to when I get a little older and start writing myself.